THEMES for early years
PHOTO... ...ABLES

SCIENCE

EDITOR

Susan Howard

ASSISTANT EDITOR

Lesley Sudlow

ILLUSTRATOR

Cathy Hughes

COVER

Lynne Joesbury

SERIES DESIGNER

Sarah Rock

DESIGNER

Rachael Hammond

AUTHOR

Jenni Tavener

For Michelle and Helen

Published by Scholastic Ltd,
Villiers House, Clarendon Avenue,
Leamington Spa, Warwickshire CV32 5PR

© 1999 Scholastic Ltd Text © 1999 Jenni Tavener

British Library Cataloguing-in-Publication Data
A catalogue record for this book is available from the British Library.

ISBN 0 439 01709 2

CONTENTS

WATER

MINIBEASTS

MATERIALS

INTRODUCTION

Using themes

The *Themes for Early Years Photocopiables* series is designed to supplement and build on the existing *Themes for Early Years* series. *Science* is divided into five chapters covering the popular themes of *Growing; Animals; Water; Minibeasts* and *Materials*.

Each chapter offers a range of activities which link directly with these theme headings. The activities offer clear links with QCA's Early Learning Goals, comprehensively covering the six areas of learning identified in the document. Many of the activities can also be used to help children to develop communication and social skills such as listening, sharing, co-operating and teamwork.

One of the enjoyable aspects of using a theme is that it gives children a sense of purpose to their activities. As the children work together on a project, they will have a reason for sharing their views and ideas with others. They will also have a focus, in terms of developing links between home and school/nursery. The children can involve their parents at home, in seeking books, pictures or artefacts related to the theme. These can then be shown to the children's peers in school/nursery, with the knowledge that there is likely to be a collective interest in their contributions.

How to use this book

Each activity chapter within this book consists of three pages of teachers' notes followed by fifteen photocopiable activities.

The activities in this book are linked with QCA's Early Learning Goals. They cover the six areas of learning and each learning objective corresponds with the QCA document. The teachers' notes explain how to use the photocopiable sheet and the resources needed to complete the activity. When appropriate, this section also includes ideas for ways to simplify the task for younger children and to extend it for older or more able children.

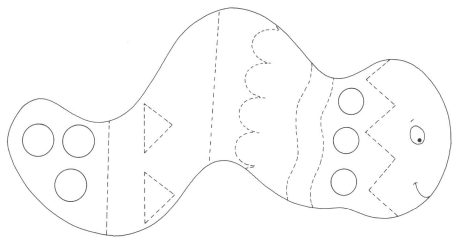

Using photocopiables

Each photocopiable sheet provides a free-standing activity. Many of the sheets can be adapted by enlarging them on the photocopier.

A variety of different approaches are used to inspire an enthusiasm for the five science themes. For example, some photocopiable sheets can be used to introduce role-play such as 'Jewels on the crown' on page 92 and 'Imaginary minibeasts' on page 74. Some can be turned into games, for example 'Animal dominoes' on page 28 and 'Honey-bee puppet' on page 73; or booklets such as 'Minibeast hunt' on page 72 and 'Minibeast story book' on page 68. Many finished photocopiable sheets can be used to create interactive displays or unusual mobiles.

Using a wide variety of resources

All the activities within this book make use of resources which are readily available in most early years environments, such as paper, card, coloured pens and pencils, paints and printing materials, a water tray, sand, collage materials, glue, scissors, dice and display boards.

They also make use of resources which can usually be found outside or in the local area such as leaves, flowers, twigs and petals. **NB:** Be aware of plants which should not be picked, such as wild flowers or plants which might cause skin irritation. Use information books to check if you are unsure yourself.

Assessment

The photocopiable sheets can be used as an assessment tool to demonstrate your coverage of the curriculum. Date and keep copies of some of the sheets once the children have completed them. Add your own notes on the reverse of the sheets, then add them to the children's personal records.

Links with home

It is important to encourage a positive liaison between home and school or nursery. An effective way of initiating this liaison is by introducing 'Home links' activities, so that children can take photocopiable sheets home to complete with their parents or carers which are relevant to the theme being covered. Many of the photocopiable sheets within this book are suitable as 'Home links' activity sheets. Some sheets which involve creating booklets, game cards and game boards could be completed at school/nursery and then taken home to share with parents and siblings.

GROWING

PAGE 10
LITTLE HANDS KEEPSAKE

Read the poem on the photocopiable sheet to the children and talk about what it means. Invite the children to look at their own hands and compare them to yours. Talk about how the size of our hands changes as we grow up.

Help each child to print both hands on their sheet using washable paint. When dry, help them to cut out their print, glue it onto card, and tape a loop of wool or ribbon to the top, so it can be hung on the wall.

Invite the children to give their 'keepsake' to someone special.

arning jective
gain vareness of e changes ich occur as e grow. ersonal, Social d Emotional velopment). oup size all groups.

PAGE 11
CLIMBING ROSE

Give each child a copy of the photocopiable sheet and encourage them to colour in and cut out the sections. Ask the children to take it in turns to lay down one picture at a time, making sure that one end of their stem matches onto the stem of the previous picture, and the other end of their stem is left clear for the next person. The aim of the activity is to use all the cards to make one long 'climbing rose' picture.

Invite the children to play the game again or to stick their 'climbing rose' onto a long sheet of paper to make an interesting picture.

arning jective
play and rk as part of eam. ersonal, Social d Emotional velopment) oup size to three ldren.

PAGE 12
NOW I AM BIG

Provide each child with a copy of the photocopiable sheet. Read the words to them. Encourage them to have a go at the activities in each box. Younger children might need a name card and a number line to help them.

Invite older children to include their surname, to use a mirror for the self-portrait and to write numbers above 10. Praise every child's efforts, and invite them to colour in the smiley face for good work.

Learning objectives
To create a personal achievement record; to boost self-confidence. (Personal, Social and Emotional Development) **Group size** Individuals or groups.

PAGES 13 AND 14
THE THREE BEARS

Enlarge the photocopiable sheet showing Mummy and Daddy Bear to A3-size. Provide each child with a picture of either Mummy, Daddy or Baby Bear to colour in and cut out. Help the children to glue their picture onto card, then punch a hole where indicated. Help them to thread a piece of wool or string through the hole and to tie it in a loop to create a dangling 'puppet'. Read or tell the story of 'The Three Bears'. Talk about how Baby Bear might have felt, and how Mummy and Daddy bear could comfort him. Encourage the children to use their puppets for imaginative play or to retell the story in their own words.

Learning objectives
To explore the roles of 'youngster' and 'grown-up'; to inspire spoken language. (Personal and Social Development/ Language and Literacy) **Group size** Three children.

PAGE 15
WORDSEARCH

Give each child a copy of the photocopiable sheet. Encourage the children to look at the words and pictures in the boxes at the bottom of the sheet and help them to read the words. Now invite them to look carefully at the grid to find each word, colouring them in as they find them.

Allow older children a high degree of independence as they complete the sheet in their own time.

Help younger children to find the initial letter of each word. Then encourage them to find the rest of the word by themselves.

PAGE 16
TEDDY TAPE-MEASURE

Give each child a copy of the photocopiable sheet and help them to colour in and cut out the two strips of teddy bears. Provide each child with a strip of card (40 x 16cm), and help them to stick the teddies onto the card to produce a teddy bear tape-measure.

Let the children lay their tape-measure beside objects in the room, and count how many teddies long they are. Provide challenges for older children such as, 'Can you find something longer than four teddies?; 'Can you find something shorter than eight teddies'; 'Can you find something the same length as five teddies?'.

Let younger children make a shorter tape-measure.

PAGE 17
TALL FLOWERS, SHORT FLOWERS

Give each child a copy of the photocopiable sheet and help them to colour in and cut out the pictures. Encourage them to mix and match the flower heads to the stems to create flowers of different heights. Can they make a tall flower and a shorter flower? Can they make two flowers the same size? Introduce terms such as tallest, shortest, taller, shorter, equal to, the same as, longer, longest and so on.

Complete the activity by helping the children to mount their flowers on backing paper to create a 'flower bed' or 'flower border' display.

PAGE 18
JACK'S BEANSTALK

Give each child a copy of the photocopiable sheet and invite them to colour in and cut out the beanstalk. Help them to write their name in the box that Jack is holding. Provide help to secure the bottom of each child's beanstalk on the wall (or display board) so that it touches the floor.

Now ask the children to stand next to their own beanstalk. Mark their height by holding a pen or your hand against the wall, then invite the children to position the top of their beanstalk in line with the mark. Let them fill in the gap using strips of green paper to create a beanstalk which matches their own height.

Help older children measure their beanstalk using a tape-measure. Let younger children use arbitrary units.

PAGE 19
GROWING UP

Provide each child with a copy of the photocopiable sheet and encourage them to look carefully at the pictures. Talk about the order in which they occur. Explain that the first picture should show the youngest child and the last picture should show a child who is about their own age. Invite the children to colour in the pictures before cutting them out. Allow older children a high degree of independence as they glue the pictures into the correct order. Younger children will need help during the sorting and cutting stages.

PAGE 20
LIFE CYCLE BOOK

**arning
jective**
compile a
ok to illustrate
e life cycle of
rog.
nowledge and
derstanding
the World)
oup size
all groups.

If possible, obtain some tadpoles so that the children can observe them changing into frogs at first hand. Alternatively, use picture books to help explain the sequence of events.

Give each child a copy of the photocopiable sheet and invite them to cut out the pictures and to place them in order along a strip of paper. Help them to bend and secure the strip of paper into a band to create a 'roundabout' picture book. The book illustrates the continuous life cycle of a frog: the frog lays frogspawn; the frogspawn hatches into tadpoles, the tadpoles grow into frogs; the frogs lay frogspawn.

PAGE 21
THERE'S A TINY CATERPILLAR

**arning
jective**
construct a
zag book to
in an
areness
out the life
le of a
tterfly.
nowledge and
derstanding
the World)
oup size
all groups.

Read the story *The Very Hungry Caterpillar* by Eric Carle (Hamish Hamilton). Talk about how a caterpillar turns into a chrysalis and then into a butterfly. Give each child a copy of the photocopiable sheet and invite them to colour it in. Help them to cut along the lines to create four pictures. Help the children to stick the pictures in order along a strip of paper, and to fold the paper to form a zigzag book.

Let older children write their name and a title on their book. Scribe the words for younger children or help them to copy write.

PAGE 22
FRUIT, GLORIOUS FRUIT!

**arning
jective**
use fine motor
ls to make a
up display.
ysical
velopment)
oup size
all or large
ups.

Talk about different fruits with the children and ask them to tell you which are their favourites. Explain how and where they are grown. If possible, take the children to see real fruit trees and plants. Alternatively, have some picture books available.

Display a real banana, apple, strawberry and orange for the children to see, touch and smell. Give each child a copy of the photocopiable sheet and encourage them to colour or paint the fruit on their sheet and to cut out their picture. Help them to draw a 'giant' fruit bowl onto a large sheet of paper, and to decorate it using apple prints.

Let each child add their fruit picture to the 'bowl' to create a group display showing a giant bowl of fruit.

PAGE 23
PRETTY BLOSSOM

Learning objective
To create a picture using a range of materials and tools.
(Creative Development)
Group size
Small groups.

Take the children outside to look at some real trees in blossom, or look at pictures in books. Invite the children to ask questions. Have a few information books nearby in case unexpected questions arise!

Provide each child with a copy of the photocopiable sheet and a selection of wax crayons in shades of pink and white. Encourage each child to cover their branch in pink or white blossom.

Help the children to mix a watery blue paint to lightly brush or sponge over the whole picture to represent sky. The paint will not stick to the wax crayon, and so will create a unique effect for each picture.

PAGE 24
BIRTHDAY CARD

Learning objective
To express ideas and stimulate creative imagination while decorating a birthday card.
(Creative Development)
Group size
Small groups.

Provide each child with a copy of the photocopiable sheet. Invite them to colour in the writing and to decorate the balloon using coloured pens, paints or collage materials, such as fabric, shiny paper, ribbons and sticky paper. Alternatively, let them use printing materials to create shapes and patterns on the balloon, or make a simple decoupage design using pictures cut out from magazines.

When complete, help the children to cut out their picture and to stick it on to the front of a sheet of folded card.

Let older children have a go at writing their own message inside their card. Younger children will need you to scribe the words for them.

Little hands keepsake

◆ Print your hands for someone special.

✂ --

Little handprints everywhere, on the tables on the chairs.

Little handprints, now let me think, on the taps and on the sink.

Little handprints everyday, just for you to wipe away.

But as I grow, you will find, no more handprints left behind.

So I've made some prints for you, of little hands, one and two.

Now, when I'm big, you'll still see, little handprints left by me!

Climbing rose

◆ Colour in and cut out the pictures. Match the stems together.

Now I am big

◆ Now I am big I can...

Write my name _____

Draw a picture of myself	Write my age

I am

_____

years old

Write some numbers	Colour in

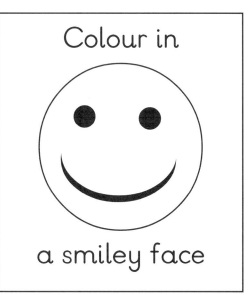

a smiley face

The three bears (1)

◆ Colour in and cut out Baby Bear.

The three bears (2)

◆ Colour in and cut out Mummy and Daddy Bear.

✂

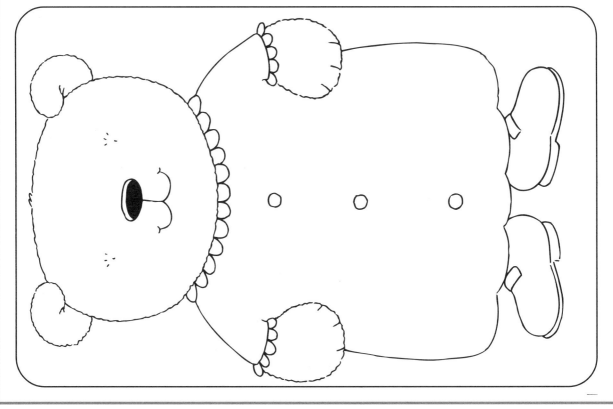

Wordsearch

◆ Look for the words and colour them in when you have found them.

p	e	o	p	l	e	x
z	x	z	w	z	x	w
a	n	i	m	a	l	s
x	z	w	x	z	x	w
f	r	u	i	t	z	x
f	l	o	w	e	r	s
t	r	e	e	s	x	z

fruit

animals

trees

flowers

people

Teddy tape-measure

◆ Colour in the teddy bears and cut into two strips. Stick onto card.

Tall flowers, short flowers

◆ Colour in and cut out the pictures. Make a tall flower and a short flower, or two flowers the same size.

Jack's beanstalk

◆ Colour in and cut out the picture. Add more paper to make it as tall as you.

Name:

Growing up

◆ Colour in the pictures. Cut them out and put them in the correct order.

Life cycle book

◆ Colour in and cut out the pictures. Put them in order from tadpole to frog.

There's a tiny caterpillar

◆ Colour in and cut out the pictures. Put them in order to make a zigzag book.

Fruit, glorious fruit!

◆ Decorate the fruit with pens or paints and then cut it out.

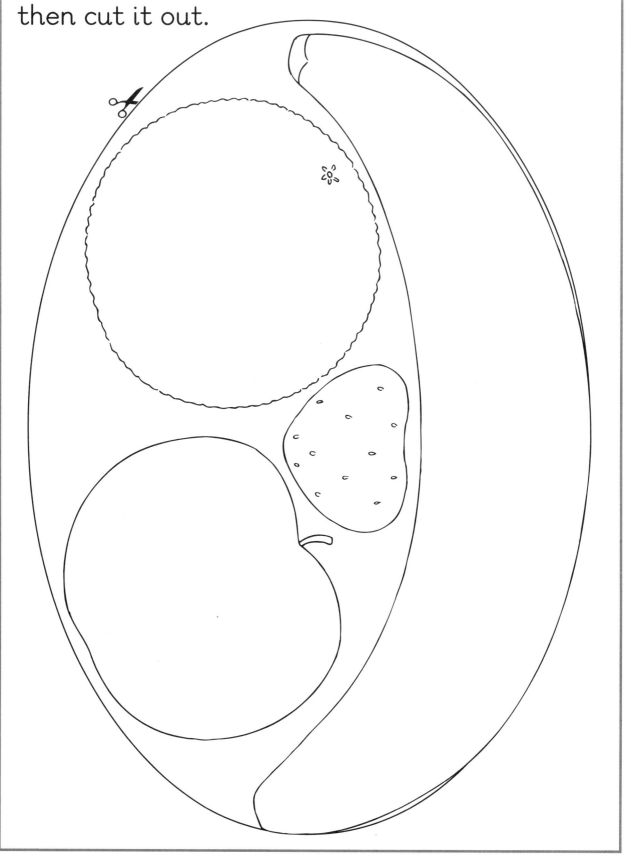

Pretty blossom

◆ Use pink or white crayons to make blossom. Use light blue paint for the sky.

Birthday card

◆ Make patterns or pictures on the balloon, colour in the writing, and then cut it out.

ANIMALS

ANIMAL DOMINOES

Learning objective
To play as part of a group to encourage co-operation and teamwork. (Personal, Social and Emotional Development)
Group size
Pairs or small groups.

Give each child a copy of the photocopiable sheet and invite them to identify and colour in the animal faces. Stick the sheet onto card and laminate it if possible. Help the children to cut carefully along the lines.

Invite the children to use the picture cards to play a simple version of dominoes. They can use any number of cards to play the game.

Help older children to adapt a second copy of the photocopiable sheet by cutting out the individual faces and rearranging them onto small rectangles of card to create a new set of dominoes.

For younger children, enlarge the sheet to make giant dominoes to use as a floor game.

PUSSY'S IN THE WELL

Learning objective
To think about the needs and feelings of others. (Personal, Social and Emotional Development)
Group size
Small groups.

Sing the nursery rhyme 'Ding Dong Bell' with the children. Give each child a copy of the photocopiable sheet and invite them to colour in the pictures. Help them to cut carefully along the lines, and then to glue the pictures onto card. Trim away any excess card for the children and cut two slits where indicated. Help the children to position the 'push up' and 'push down' between the slits in the well.

Encourage the children to move the strip up and down to make Pussy go in and out of the well. Discuss how Pussy must have felt. Talk about the need to be kind to animals, and about how we can help animals to keep safe.

ANIMAL CROSSWORD

Give each child a copy of the photocopiable sheet and ask them to look at the animal pictures. Help them to sound out the letters and read the words. Explain that the letters on the crossword match the first letter of each animal. Show them an example such as 'd' for 'dog'. Encourage older children to have a go at finding and writing the correct words by themselves. Help younger children by saying each initial sound while pointing to the shape of the letter.

Learning objective
To develop writing, reading and word matching skills. (Language and Literacy).
Group size
Small groups.

BIRD PUPPETS

Say the rhyme 'Two little dicky-birds' with the children. Give each child a copy of the photocopiable sheet and ask them to colour in the two birds in two different colours. Let them decide who is 'Peter' and who is 'Paul'. Help them to cut along the lines and to make a hole in the top of each picture using a hole punch. Add reinforcement rings to prevent the holes from tearing. Help the children to thread some wool through each hole, then invite them to hold and manoeuvre both puppets while singing the rhyme.

Learning objective
To make and use simple puppets to use as props while singing rhymes. (Language and Literacy)
Group size
Small groups.

PATCHWORK ELEPHANT

Read some of the *Elmer the Elephant* stories by David McKee (Andersen Press). Give each child a copy of the photocopiable sheet and help them to colour the code on their sheet, and then to follow the code to decorate the elephant. Ask them to sound out the letters and to read the colour words when they refer to their code.

Learning objective
To match initial letter sounds and to begin to recognize colour words. (Language and Literacy)
Group size
Small groups.

When the sheets are complete, invite each child to cut out the picture of the elephant along the thick, black line. Help all the children to glue their pictures in a long line to create a procession of elephants and then use as a number line by writing numbers above each elephant.

PAGE 33
OLD MACDONALD'S ANIMALS

Learning objective
To reinforce the number sequence 1 to 10 and to develop counting skills. (Mathematics)
Group size
Small groups.

Invite the whole group to paint trees, flowers, fences and so on onto a large sheet of green paper to represent Old MacDonald's farm.

Provide each child with a copy of the photocopiable sheet and invite them to use a pencil to follow the numbers 1 to 10 around each animal. Let them colour in the animals and give them a tail. Help the children to cut along the solid lines and invite the whole group to stick their animal pictures onto the 'field'. Display the picture, and ask questions such as 'How many cows are there?'; 'Are there more cows than pigs?'; 'How many animals altogether?'.

PAGE 34
RAINBOW FISH

Learning objective
To recognize numerals 1 to 6 and to follow a code. (Mathematics)
Group size
Small groups.

Give each child a copy of the photocopiable sheet and begin by encouraging the children to use six different colours to make their code.

Help them to follow their code to colour in their fish, then invite them to create a colourful display by cutting and gluing their fish onto a shiny blue background. Let them use collage materials to add seaweed, shells, bubbles and so on. Use the activity to inspire an interest in the amazing colours and patterns on tropical fish. If possible, arrange a visit to see a tank of tropical fish. Alternatively, show the children pictures and posters.

PAGE 35
FIND BABY RABBIT

Provide a copy of the photocopiable sheet for each child and encourage them to write the numbers 1, 2, 3, 5 and 8 by tracing over the dots on the sheet. Help them to identify and write the missing numbers using the number line as a guide.

Explain that the game is about a baby rabbit who has run through the vegetable patch collecting carrots, but he has dropped some on the way. To play the game, you will need one dice and a counter each placed at the Start. Take turns to throw the dice and move along the spaces. If you land on a space showing a dropped carrot you go back two spaces. The winner is the first player to find baby rabbit at the Finish.

Learning objectives
To recognize and write numbers 1 to 10; to make and play a number game. (Mathematics)
Group size
A game for one to three players.

PAGE 36
THE LOST PUPPY

Give each child a copy of the photocopiable sheet and ask them to find the position of the puppy and the owner on the map. Ask them to think of how many different ways the puppy could walk home, and to mark out each route using a different coloured pencil.

Talk about what the puppy will pass on each journey. Let older children find the longest and shortest routes.

Help younger children by asking them to begin by tracing each route with their finger. Enlarge the sheet to A3 size for group work and discussion.

Learning objective
To introduce simple map-reading skills. (Knowledge and Understanding of the World)
Group size
Small groups or individuals.

PAGE 37
HICKORY DICKORY DOCK

Give each child an A3 or A4 copy of the photocopiable sheet. Ask them to colour in the pictures, then help them to cut along the lines.

Give assistance to stick the clock onto strong card. An adult should punch a hole where indicated. Help the children to stick the mice pictures back to back and to attach them to a length of wool or string. Thread the wool through the hole in the 'clock' and tie a knot in the other end. Invite the children to pull the knot to make the

Learning objectives
To use a variety of tools to make a simple toy with moving parts; to develop co-ordinated hand movements. (Physical Development)
Group size
Small groups.

mouse run up the clock. When they let go, the mouse will run down again.

Encourage the children to sing 'Hickory Dickory Dock' as they move the mouse up and down the clock.

PAGE 38
GIVE A DOG A BONE

Learning objective
To develop pre-writing and co-ordination skills. (Physical Development)
Group size
Individuals or small groups.

Give each child a copy of the photocopiable sheet and a sharp pencil. Encourage them to follow the dotted lines carefully, in the direction of the arrows. Invite them to colour in the animals and to identify the type of food they eat. Encourage the children to talk about other animals within their experience, and the different types of food and drink they need, for example pets, animals they have seen in the countryside, in pet shops or in zoos.

PAGE 39
ANIMAL SHAPES GAME

Learning objective
To develop gross motor skills and spatial awareness. (Physical Development)
Group size
Small or large groups.

Enlarge the photocopiable sheet to A3 size. Cut out the circle and spinner arm and attach together using a paper fastener. Display the spinner in a room with music facilities and enough space for the children to move around safely.

Invite the children to hop like a rabbit, wriggle like a worm, walk like a puppy or flap like a bird, in time with the music. When the music stops, the children should 'freeze' in the shape of the animal they were imitating. Spin the spinner arm. Everyone doing the movement that matches the animal is 'out'. Play until there is a winner.

Encourage younger children to play for fun, with everyone joining in again after each spin. Invite older children to make the spinner, and to take turns controlling the music and spinner.

PAGE 40
FIVE LITTLE DUCKS MOBILE

Learning objective
To handle objects with increasing control. (Creative Development)
Group size
Five children.

Give each child a photocopiable sheet and invite them to decorate the duck. Supply a range of resources such as paints, crayons, felt-tipped pens, pastels and collage materials.

Supervise the children as they cut along the lines, and make two holes where indicated. Help them to thread wool or string through both holes, then tie them together with the other ducks to make a long mobile.

Invite older children to use two sheets each and to glue both ducks back to back. Let them thread their own string or wool through the holes and work out how to tie the ducks together. Younger children will need help with threading and tying.

PAGE 41
WISE OLD OWL

Learning objective
To explore shape, colour and texture in two and three dimensions. (Creative Development)
Group size
Small groups.

Read *Goodnight, Owl* by Pat Hutchins (Puffin) or another story which includes an owl. Give each child a copy of the photocopiable sheet to colour in or collage. Help them to cut out the pieces and stick them onto card.

Ask the children to help you attach the wings to the owl using paper fasteners, so that they 'flap'.

If possible, take the children outside to find a long stick or branch. Alternatively, let them paint a cardboard tube brown. Invite the group to use strong adhesive tape to secure their owls in a row along the branch.

Hang the branch in front of a dark blue background, speckled with shiny stars and a moon to create a unusual 3-D display.

PAGE 42
SOFT TOY PET

Learning objective
To design and make a toy using a range of materials. (Creative Development)
Group size
Individuals.

Give each child an A4 or A3 copy of the photocopiable sheet. Help them to cut around the thick, black line to create a paper pattern, and to pin the pattern onto a piece of non-fraying fabric, such as felt.

Assist the children in cutting out two fabric shapes and gluing or sewing around the edge leaving a small gap for stuffing. Supervise the children as they carefully place a small amount of soft toy stuffing into the gap.

Help them to sew or glue the gap together and to cut out and glue felt or string features such as eyes, nose, mouth, ears, whiskers and tails onto their soft toy.

Animal dominoes

◆ Colour in the animals. Cut along the lines to make dominoes.

Pussy's in the well

◆ Colour in the pictures, then cut them out and stick them onto card.

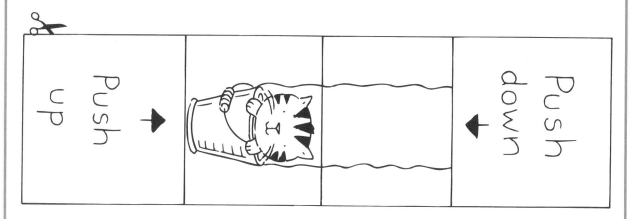

Animal crossword

◆ Write the names of the animals in the crossword. Look at the first letter of each animal to help you.

dog

pig

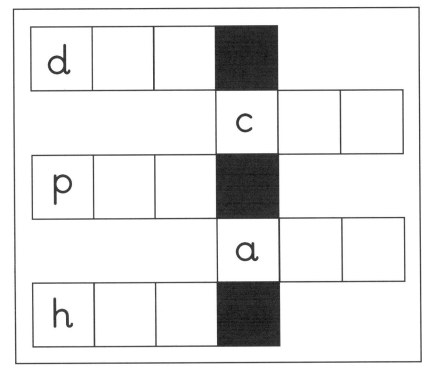

cat

hen

ant

Bird puppets

◆ Colour in the pictures and cut along the lines. Make a hole in each picture to hang a thread.

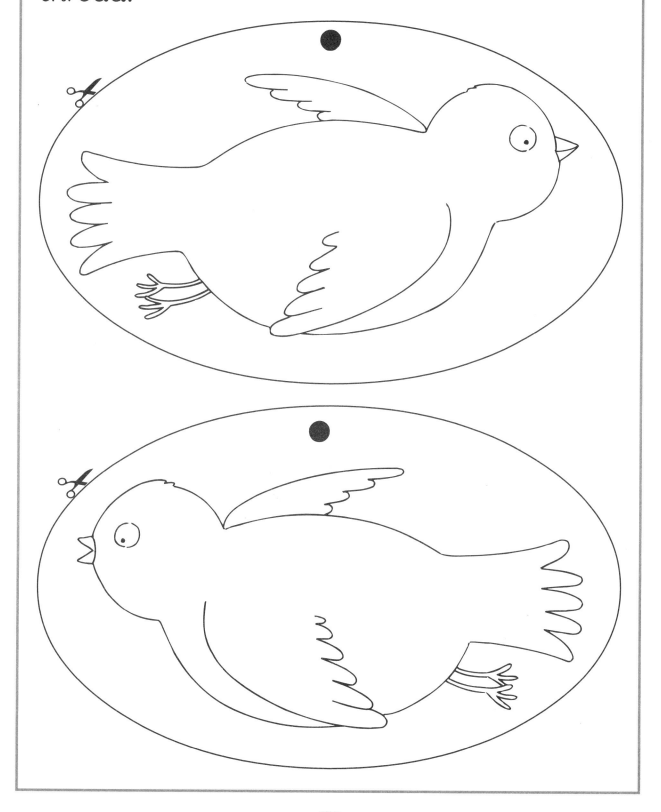

Patchwork elephant

◆ Follow the code to colour the elephant.

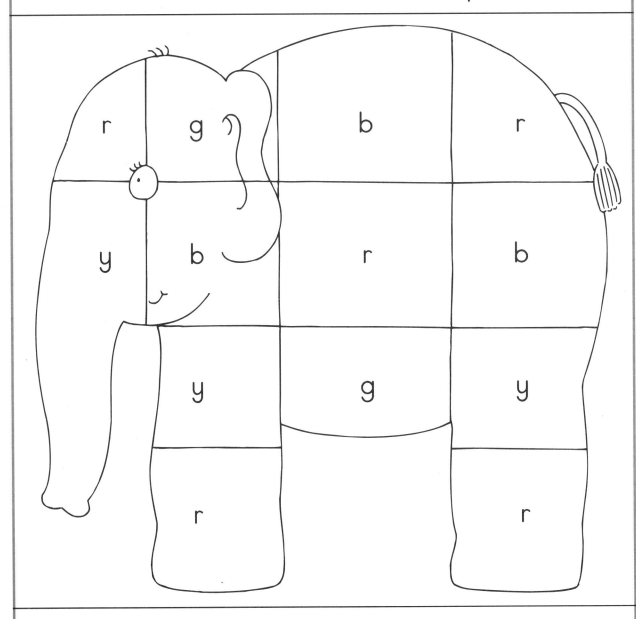

Colour code

r → red   b → blue

g → green   y → yellow

Old MacDonald's animals

◆ Use a pencil to follow the numbers from 1 to 10. Colour in the animals and give them each a tail.

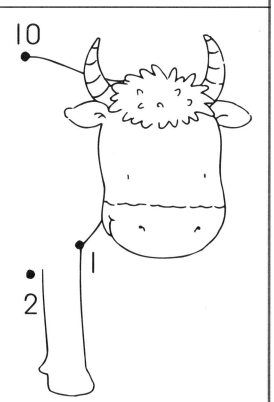

Rainbow fish

◆ Make up your own colour code. Follow your code to colour the fish.

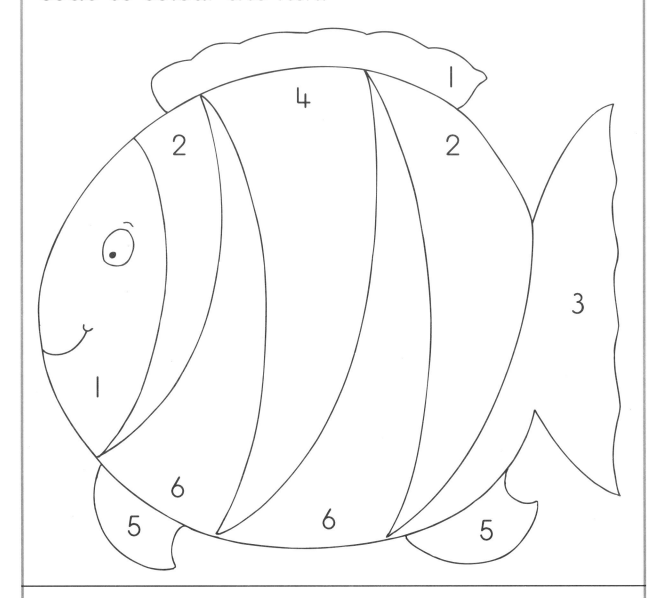

Colour code

1 = ◯   2 = ◯   3 = ◯

4 = ◯   5 = ◯   6 = ◯

Find baby rabbit

◆ Use the number line to help you write the numbers 1 to 10, then play the game.

Number line

| 1 | 2 | 3 | 4 | 5 | 6 | 7 | 8 | 9 | 10 |

Finish

The lost puppy

◆ Draw lines to show how many different ways the puppy could walk home.

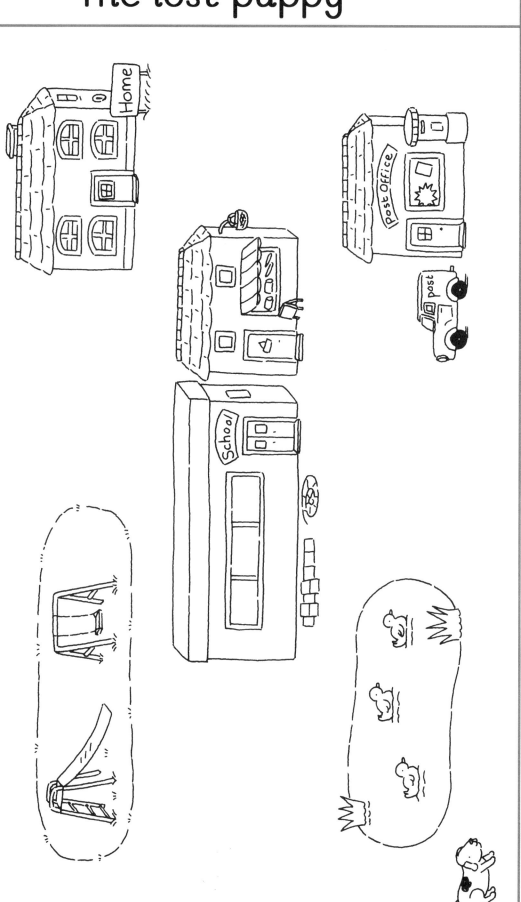

Hickory dickory dock

◆ Colour in and cut out the pictures.

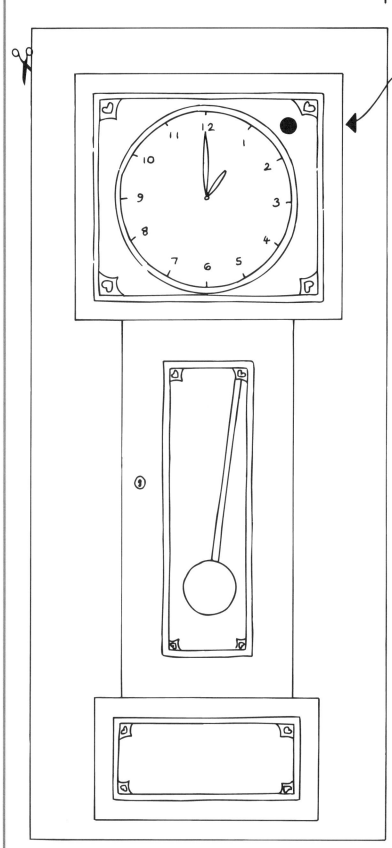

Hole for thread.

Front.

Back.

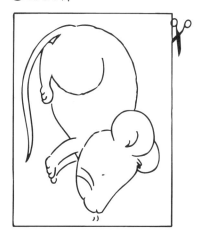

Tape thread
to mouse.

Give a dog a bone

◆ Use a pencil to follow the dotted lines.

Animal shapes game

◆ Make a spinner.

wriggle   walk

hop   flap

Spinner arm

Five little ducks mobile

◆ Cut along the lines. Decorate your duck.

Wise old owl

◆ Colour in and cut out the parts of the owl. Attach the wings to the owl using paper fasteners.

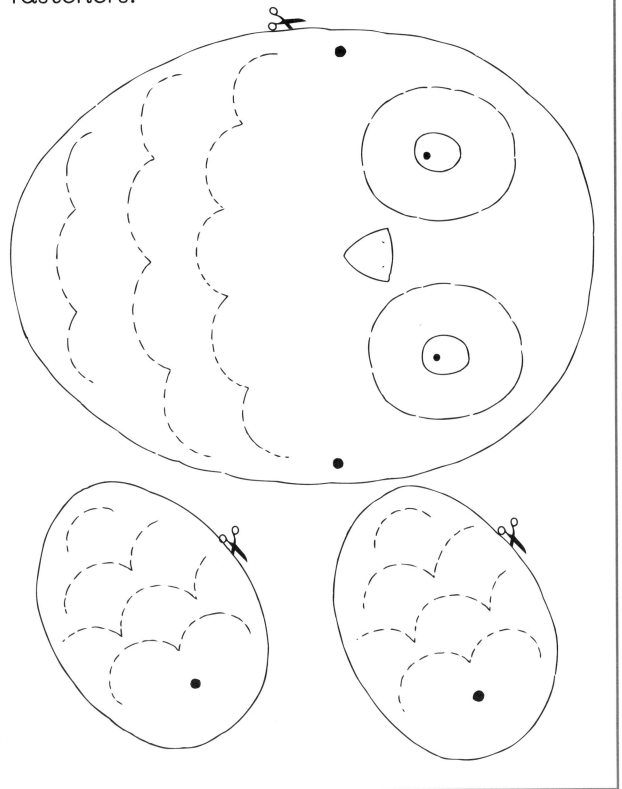

Soft toy pet

◆ Cut out the shape. Make your own toy from fabric.

Some toy pet ideas.

Leave a gap for stuffing.

WATER

PAGE 46
OUR SOUP RECIPE

Learning objectives
To take turns and share fairly; to record a set of ingredients for others to use. (Personal, Social and Emotional Development)
Group size
Pairs or small groups with close adult supervision.

Ask the children to wash their hands and put on a clean apron. Invite them to help you wash and prepare a selection of vegetables to make soup. To avoid the use of sharp tools, provide vegetables which can be torn, broken or snapped by hand, such as broccoli, cauliflower, spinach or peas/beans from pods.

Invite the children to place the prepared vegetables into a pan of cold water or cooled vegetable stock. An adult should supervise the cooking stage by placing the pan on the heat source to simmer until the vegetables are soft.

When the soup is ready, let it cool then invite the children to share it out.

Provide each child with a copy of the photocopiable sheet. Invite the children to draw the vegetables they used in the space around the edge of their sheet. Encourage older children to 'have a go' at writing the ingredients in the centre of the sheet and scribe the words for younger children.

Place each recipe page into a plastic wallet and clip together in an A4 file. Use these as the first pages of the children's own recipe file.

PAGE 47
WHAT DO THEY NEED?

Learning objective
To encourage an awareness of the needs of others. (Personal, Social and Emotional Development)
Group size
Individuals or small groups.

Give each child a copy of the photocopiable sheet and encourage them to identify the items in the four small pictures. Ask them to explain what is happening in the four main pictures. Encourage them to talk about what each person needs and why.

Help the children to cut along the dotted lines and to stick the four small pictures in the correct positions. Invite them to colour in their picture.

PAGE 48
BUBBLES POEM

Learning objective
To inspire descriptive and poetic language. (Language and Literacy)
Group size
Individuals, small or large groups.

Invite the children to blow some bubbles into the air. Encourage them to describe what they see. Provide each child with a copy of the photocopiable sheet. Ask older children to have a go at writing one word in each bubble picture to describe their real bubbles. You will need to scribe the words for younger children, or write them for the children to copy.

Alternatively, enlarge the sheet to A3 and use as a group activity.

Encourage the children to read their work including the pre-printed words to create a rhyming poem. For example, 'Bubbles, bubbles everywhere... floating, pretty, colours, popping ... in the air'.

PAGE 49
RAIN, RAIN, GO AWAY

Learning objectives
To develop counting skills with numbers from 1 to 8; to encourage number writing practice. (Mathematics)
Group size
Individuals or small groups.

Provide each child with a copy of the photocopiable sheet. Invite them to write their name on the line, within the words of the rhyme, then read the whole rhyme to them.

Encourage the children to count the raindrops in the different parts of the picture and to write the answers in the boxes. Invite them to refer to the number line in order to write the numbers correctly.

PAGE 50
WASHING LINE GAME

Learning objective
To reinforce an understanding of number values. (Mathematics)
Group size
A game for two to three players.

Give each child a copy of the photocopiable game sheet and a crayon. Provide a dice, showing the figures 1 to 6, for the group. Ask the children to take turns to throw the dice, then to colour in the item of clothing that matches the number they have thrown. If the matching item is

already coloured in, then that player should pass the dice on. The winner is the first child to colour in all six items of clothing on their game sheet.

Simplify the game for younger children by providing a dice showing dots 1 to 6. Older children can use a dice showing the words 'one' to 'six'.

PAGE 51
SHIP SHAPE!

Learning objective
To identify different shapes and to encourage counting and matching skills. (Mathematics)
Group size
Small groups.

Give each child a copy of the photocopiable sheet. Encourage the children to look carefully at the picture and to count how many triangles, squares, circles and oblongs they can find. Ask them to write each answer under the matching shape at the bottom of the page.

Challenge older children by adding more shapes to the picture using a black felt-tipped pen. Provide younger children with a number line showing 1 to 5, to help them identify and write the correct numbers.

PAGE 52
WATER SEARCH

Learning objective
To investigate objects in their everyday lives. (Knowledge and Understanding of the World)
Group size
Individuals or small groups.

Provide each child with a copy of the photocopiable sheet. Talk with the children about what they can see in each room on the sheet. Ask them to identify things which hold water and to record their observations by drawing a circle around them. Talk about the wide variety of uses we have for water in our homes.

Extend the activity for older children by asking parents to help their child record, in words or pictures, things in their own home which hold water.

PAGE 53
UNDER, ON OR ABOVE?

Provide each child with a copy of the photocopiable sheet. Help them to cut along the lines and to identify the six pictures. Talk with the children about which of the animals and machines go under, on or above the water. Encourage them to sort and stick the pictures in the correct position on the main scene.

Invite the children to colour in their finished picture.

PAGE 54
RAINBOW COLOURS

Provide each child with a copy of the photocopiable sheet to colour in. Explain what each colour says on the rainbow. Encourage them to follow the dotted lines in the direction of the arrows and to write the words 'sun' and 'rain'. Help them to cut around their picture and to stick it onto card. Provide crayons or pencils in the seven colours of the rainbow, and invite older children to draw a free-hand rainbow on the reverse side. Younger children can draw patterns.

An adult should punch a hole in the top of the picture. Help the children to thread wool or string through the hole and hang up to create a mobile.

PAGES 55 AND 56
CATCH THE SEA CREATURES!

Make enlarged copies of the photocopiable sheets on pages 55 and 56. Invite the children to use paints, pastels or felt-tipped pens to colour in the sea creatures.

Cut both sheets as indicated. Position the pictures from Part 1 in the four corners of the room, making sure there is enough space for the children to move around freely and safely. Place the pictures from Part 2 in a pile face down. Play some music and encourage the children to move around the room. Suggest ways of moving which reflect the sea creature theme, such as walking sideways like a crab, swimming fast or

Learning objective
To talk about features of the everyday world and to encourage decision making (Knowledge and Understanding of the World)
Group size
Small groups.

Learning objective
To find out about features of the natural world and to use these findings to colour in a picture. (Knowledge and Understanding of the World)
Group size
Small groups.

Learning objective
To encourage large movements showing an awareness of space; to play safely and fairly (Physical Development)
Group size
Small groups to help make the game; whole group to play the game.

slow like fish and moving softly and gently like a jellyfish.

After a while, turn off the music, and ask the children to quickly choose one sea creature picture to sit by, as a place to hide from the fishing boat.

When the children are seated, turn over the top card from the pile to show where the fishing net has landed. All the children who are hiding in the same place have been caught by the net, and should sit out for the next round. Shuffle the cards and repeat the game.

PAGE 57
WAVES AND RIPPLES

Learning objective
To develop hand control and to practice handwriting patterns. (Physical Development)
Group size
Individuals or small groups.

Prepare for this activity by showing the children how ripples are formed. Let them drop pebbles into a bowl of water, and invite them to try to make waves in a large water tray. Provide each child with a copy of the photocopiable sheet and a blue pencil. Encourage them to follow the dotted lines carefully, in the direction of the arrows. Invite them to colour in the two pictures.

PAGE 58
ROW, ROW, ROW YOUR BOAT

Learning objective
To develop fine motor skills. (Physical Development)
Group size
Small groups.

Sing the nursery rhyme to the children. Invite them to join in with you as you sing it a second time, this time miming the actions of rowing a boat.

Provide each child with a copy of the photocopiable sheet. Using a coloured pencil, invite the children to follow each maze to find out which rowing boat is on the correct route 'to see a crocodile'.

Encourage the children to count how many fish there are along each route, and to write the answers on the matching boats.

Extend the activity for older children by adding more fish on each route for them to count.

PAGE 59
COLOUR MIXING

Provide each child with a copy of the photocopiable sheet, powder paints in primary colours only (red, blue and yellow), water and painting equipment. Invite the children to carefully mix their primary colours as indicated on the sheet to create three new secondary colours (orange, green and purple).

Help younger children to practise mixing realistic quantities of powder and water before they tackle the photocopiable sheet. Encourage older children to experiment with the paints to achieve shades of brown.

Learning objective
To explore colours and experiment creating new colours. (Creative Development)
Group size
Small groups.

PAGE 60
ICE LOLLY JIGSAW

Talk to the children about ice lollies. Explain that they are made by freezing water in a mould. Let the children observe an ice cube as it melts and slowly turns into water.

Provide each child with a copy of the photocopiable sheet. Invite them to select their own choice of coloured pens or pencils to decorate the ice lolly picture. Help them to carefully cut along the lines to create a four-piece jigsaw.

Encourage the children to assemble their jigsaw and to take turns assembling each other's jigsaws.

Challenge older children by giving them a time limit to piece together one or more jigsaws.

Learning objective
To decorate and make a simple jigsaw puzzle. (Creative Development)
Group size
Small groups.

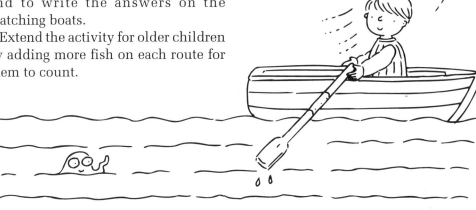

Our soup recipe

◆ Draw and write your ingredients.

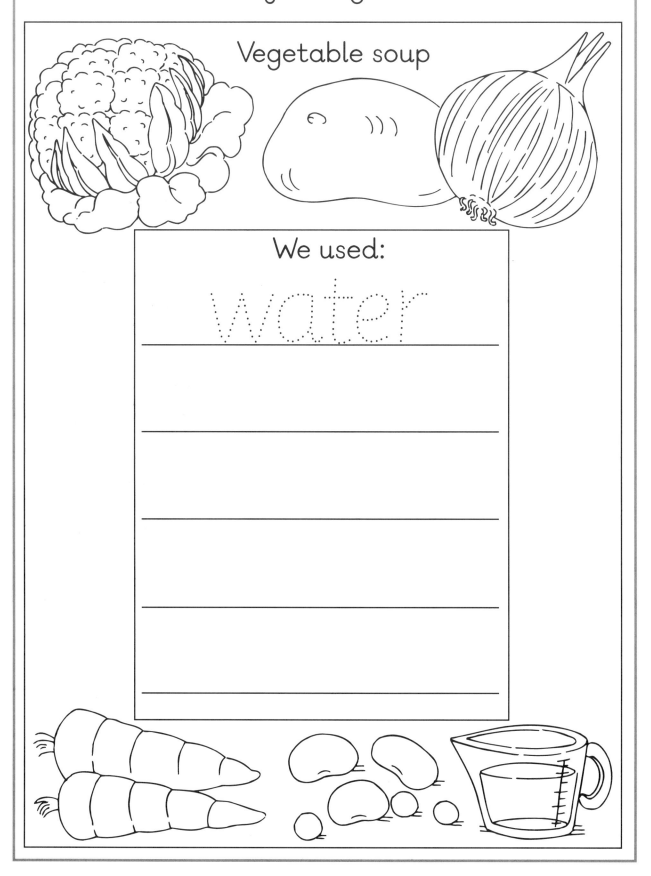

Vegetable soup

We used:

water

What do they need?

◆ Cut out the pictures and stick them in the correct spaces.

Bubbles poem

◆ Blow some bubbles. Write one word inside each bubble to describe what you see.

Bubbles, bubbles everywhere...

...in the air.

Rain, rain, go away

◆ Count the raindrops and write the answers in the correct boxes. Add your name.

| 1 | 2 | 3 | 4 | 5 | 6 | 7 | 8 |

Rain, rain, go away,
Come again
another day;

Little _____
wants to play.
Rain, rain, go away.

Washing line game

◆ Throw a dice and colour in the matching item of clothing.

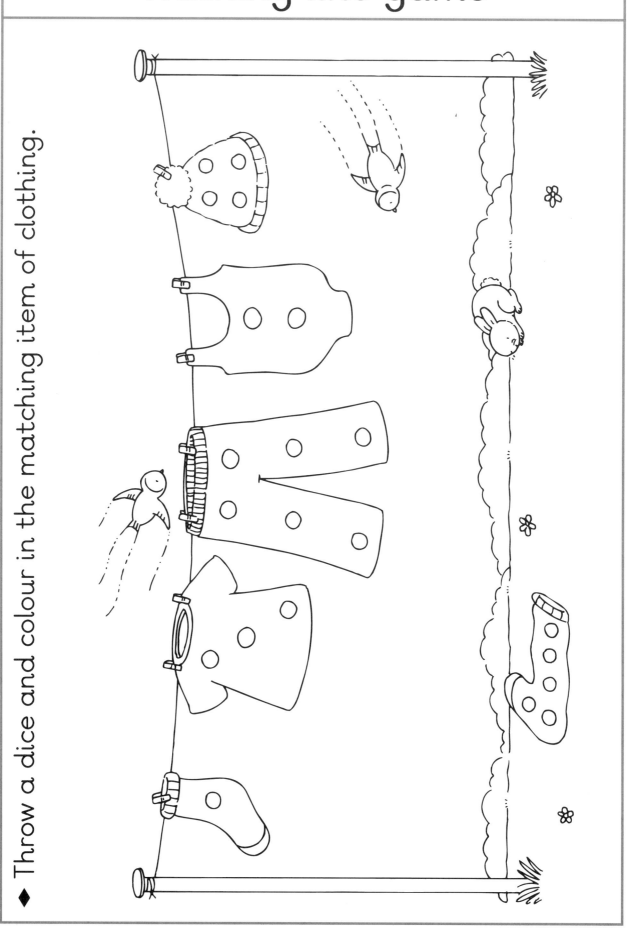

Ship shape!

◆ Count how many different shapes you can see in the picture.

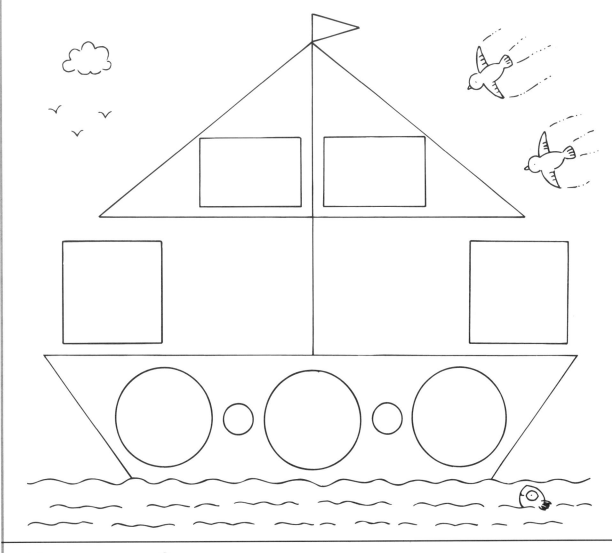

How many?

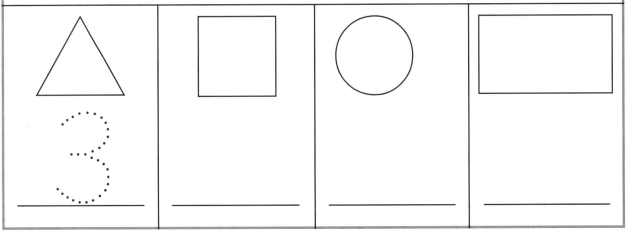

SCIENCE

51

WATER

Water search

♦ Draw a circle around all the things which hold water.

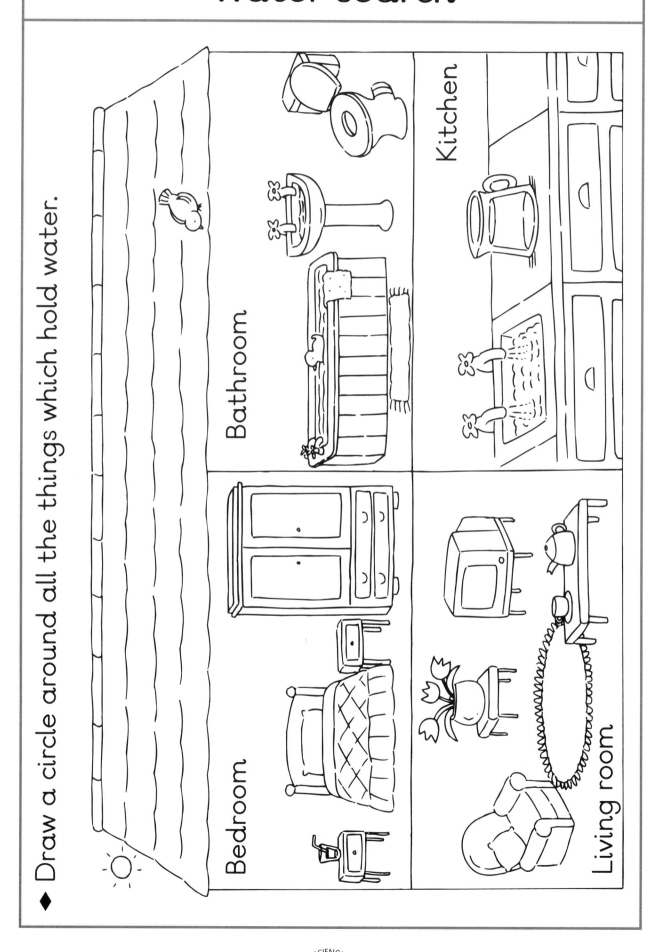

Bathroom

Kitchen

Bedroom

Living room

Under, on or above?

◆ Cut out the pictures and put them in the correct places.

Rainbow colours

◆ Colour in and cut out the picture. Write the words 'sun' and 'rain'.

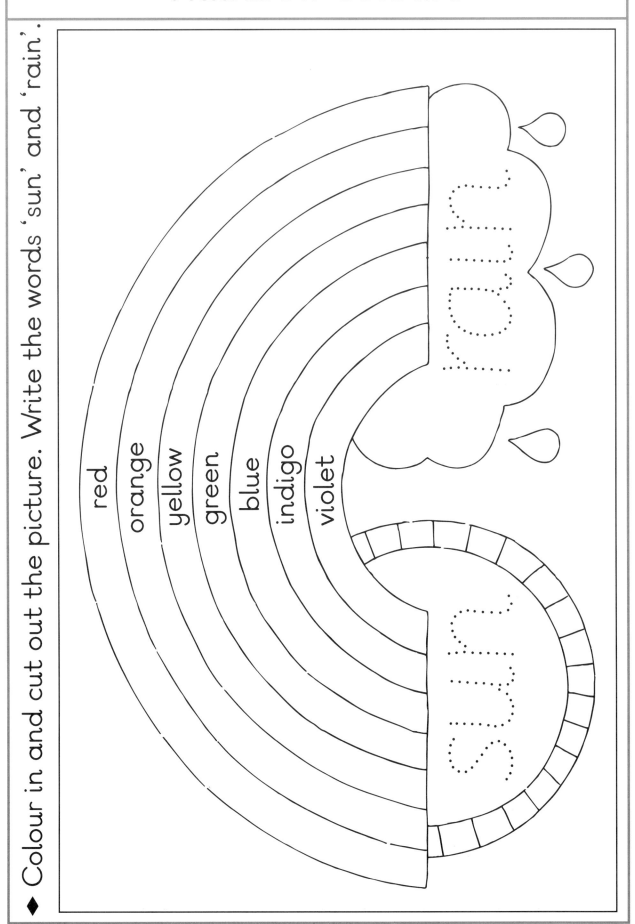

red
orange
yellow
green
blue
indigo
violet

Catch the sea creatures! (1)

◆ Colour in and cut out the game cards.

Catch the sea creatures! (2)

◆ Colour in and cut out the game cards.

Waves and ripples

◆ Use a blue pencil to follow the dotted lines.

Row, row, row your boat

◆ Follow the mazes to find out who meets the crocodile.

Row, row, row your boat,
gently down the stream.
If you see a crocodile, don't forget to scream!

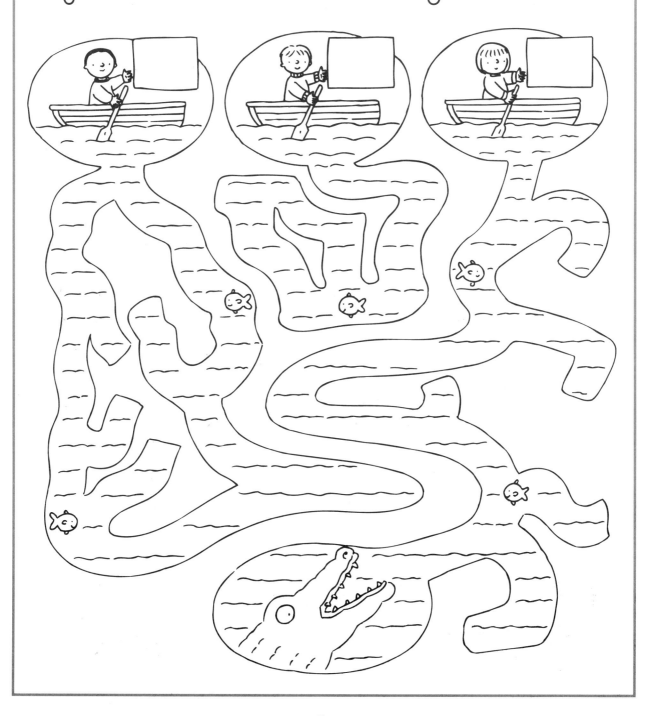

Colour mixing

◆ Use paints to mix the colours.

red

blue

yellow

purple

green

orange

blue

yellow

red

Ice lolly jigsaw

◆ Colour in the picture and cut along the lines.

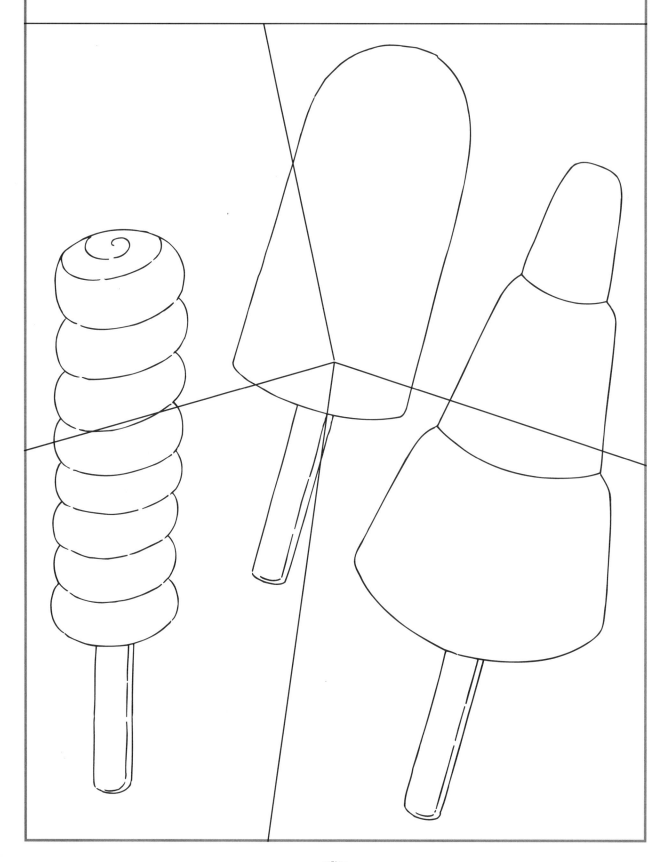

MINIBEASTS

PAGE 64
MINIBEAST GAMES

Give each child a copy of the photocopiable sheet and invite them to colour in the pictures of the minibeasts. Provide help as the children cut out the individual cards. Help them to stick the pictures onto separate sheets of card.

Ask two children to combine their picture cards to make a shared set, containing eighteen cards. Show the children how to play matching games such as 'Snap' and 'Pairs'.

Provide younger children with A3 copies of the photocopiable sheet. Help them during the cutting and sticking stages and cover the cards in plastic film to protect them from tearing.

PAGE 65
TWO LITTLE LADYBIRDS

Read the story *The Bad-Tempered Ladybird* by Eric Carle (Picture Puffin) to the children. Talk with them about feeling 'bad-tempered' and 'friendly'. Ask them if they can remember a time when someone was particularly friendly to them, or bad-tempered. What did the person do or say? How did it make the children feel?

Provide each child with a copy of the photocopiable sheet. Encourage them to write or draw about these incidents on the appropriate picture. Alternatively, invite them to draw or write about something the ladybirds did or said which was friendly and bad-tempered.

Compile the photocopiable sheets into a book about 'feelings'.

PAGE 66
BEAUTIFUL BUTTERFLY

Provide each child with a copy of the photocopiable sheet and ask them to look at the colour code at the top of the sheet. Explain that each letter matches the first sound of a colour word, for example, 'r' for 'red'.

Using felt-tipped pens or pencils in red, blue, yellow and green, invite the children to follow the code to colour in the butterfly.

PAGE 67
UGLY BUG BALL

Give each child a copy of the photocopiable sheet. Explain that it is an invitation to an 'ugly bug ball'. Ask them who they would like to invite (such as a friend or a toy) and on which day they would like the ball to be held.

Alternatively, make the invitations 'real' by arranging an ugly bug ball. This could involve the children dressing up as ugly bugs and dancing to music, or gathering together a group of ugly bug toys for the children to dance with!

Invite the children to colour their sheet. Let older children have a go at writing the invitation independently. Let younger children copy-write or scribe the words for them.

MINIBEAST STORY BOOK

Learning objective
To read simple sentences and to make their own story book. (Language and Literacy)
Group size
Individuals or small groups.

Provide each child with an A4 or A3 copy of the photocopiable sheet. Read the words to them. Encourage the children to choose a minibeast to draw 'in', 'on' and 'under' the pictures. Help them to write the words 'in', 'on' and 'under'.

Help the children to cut along the lines to make four separate sections. Punch two holes on the left-hand side of each section and let the children secure them together using treasury tags to make a four-page book.

Invite each child to write their name on the cover.

HUNGRY CATERPILLARS

Learning objective
To reinforce counting skills. (Mathematics)
Group size
A game for two to three players.

Read the story *The Very Hungry Caterpillar* by Eric Carle (Hamish Hamilton) to the children. Give each child a copy of the photocopiable sheet and help them to fill in the missing numbers on the sheet from 1 to 10.

Invite the children to cut out and colour in the three caterpillar counters using a different colour for each. To play the game, each child should place their caterpillar counter on number 1. They then take turns to throw a dice and move accordingly. The winner is the first player to reach number 10.

Invite older children to include messages on their game sheet such as 'feeling hungry, move on one space' or 'feeling ill, miss a go'!

HOW MANY SPOTS?

Learning objective
To encourage number recognition from 1 to 10. (Mathematics)
Group size
Individuals or small groups.

Provide each child with a copy of the photocopiable sheet. Invite them to count the spots on each ladybird and to write the answers in the boxes. Encourage them to refer to the number line to find out how to write each number correctly.

Ask older children to work out which numbers have not been used (1, 4, 9, 10). Ask them to draw four ladybirds on a separate sheet of paper, showing 1, 4, 9 and 10 spots.

WORMS!

Provide each child with a copy of the photocopiable sheet and several narrow strips of coloured sticky paper (approximately 1cm by 10–20cm).

Ask the children to cut or tear four strips of paper to match the length of each worm on the sheet, then to stick each strip next to the matching worm.

Encourage the children to compare the worms using simple mathematical terms such as 'longest', shortest', 'bigger than', smaller than', 'the same size as' and so on.

Extend the activity for older children by asking them to measure and record the length of each worm in centimetres.

Help younger children to use arbitrary units, such as building bricks, to measure each worm. Encourage the children to write each length on the appropriate strips of paper.

MINIBEAST HUNT

Take the children on a 'minibeast hunt' in a safe place where they can look under logs, bushes, long grass, small stones and so on for tiny creatures.

Give each child an A4 or A3 copy of the photocopiable sheet to record information about a minibeast seen during the 'hunt'. Encourage them to draw pictures in the boxes showing the minibeast and where they found it. Invite older children to write the name of the minibeast and a word or sentence to describe it under the headings 'I saw' and 'It was'. Scribe the words for younger children.

HONEY-BEE PUPPET

Give each child a copy of the photocopiable sheet to colour in. Help them to cut out the bee shape, then cut out and tape tissue-paper wings and six wool legs onto their bee. Help them to secure a thread through the centre of the 'bee' to make a string puppet.

Invite the children to make some scenery by painting flowers and a

Learning objective
To devel... matching skil... compariso... a... mathematic... languag... (Mathemati...
Group si...
Individuals small group...

Learning objectiv...
To investiga... living thir... and to reco... th... observatio... (Knowledge a... Understand... of the Wo...
Group s...
Small grou...

Learn...
object...
To think ab... the life ... living creatu... (Knowledge ... Understand... of the Wo...
Group s...
Small grou...

beehive. Mount the pictures onto folded card to make them free-standing.

Invite the children to move their bee puppets between the 'flowers' and 'hive' to reinforce their understanding of the honey-bee.

PAGE 74

IMAGINARY MINIBEASTS

Provide each child with a copy of the photocopiable sheet to decorate, and a selection of resources to use, such as glue and glitter, collage materials, paints and printing equipment, sticky and shiny paper, pastels and crayons. Encourage them to use their creative imaginations to produce an unusual mask. Help each child to make a headband for their mask from a strip of card. Attach the masks to the headband using sticky tape.

Invite the children to wear their masks while they dance, using exaggerated body movements, to music at an imaginary 'ugly bug ball'.

PAGE 75

JAZZY CATERPILLAR

Provide each child with an A4 or A3 copy of the photocopiable sheet. Encourage them to use coloured pens or pencils to follow the dotted lines on the caterpillar, in the direction of the arrows. Help them to cut around their caterpillar shape.

Cover a display board with strips of paper in shades of green to represent giant blades of grass. Invite the children to create an imaginative and colourful display by weaving their caterpillars through the blades of 'grass'.

PAGE 76

HIDING IN THE HEDGEROW

Plan this activity in advance by inviting the children to take photographs of each other or by asking parents for a spare photograph of their child.

Provide each child with a copy of the photocopiable sheet to colour in using bold, bright colours. Help them to cut out their own picture from the

photograph and to place themselves in the hedgerow scene. Help them to cut out the leaf shape and to use it as a flap to hide or partially hide their photograph.

Use the pictures to create an interactive display, with labels inviting the children to find out who is hiding behind each leaf.

PAGE 77

HONEYCOMB COLLAGE

Provide each child with an A4 or A3 copy of the photocopiable sheet. Provide a wide range of coloured pens and pencils and collage materials such as fabric, coloured paper, shiny paper, lace, textured paper, sequins, buttons and so on. Encourage the children to decorate the hexagons in different colours, patterns or by using different collage materials.

Mount each design onto folded card to create an unusual celebration card, or add a calendar onto each design to create a child-made gift to take home. Alternatively, combine several collages to create a large 'honeycomb' display.

PAGE 78

SNAILS

Provide each child with an A4 or A3 copy of the photocopiable sheet. Encourage them to follow the dotted lines on each snail, using a sharp pencil. Ask them to start in the centre and place their pencil on the dot. When complete, invite the children to use their creative imaginations to decorate the four snails using coloured pens, pencils, paints or pastels.

Make an interesting border or counting line by helping the children to cut around the boxes and displaying several snail pictures together in a line.

Minibeast games

◆ Colour in the pictures. Use them to play pairs, snap or matching games.

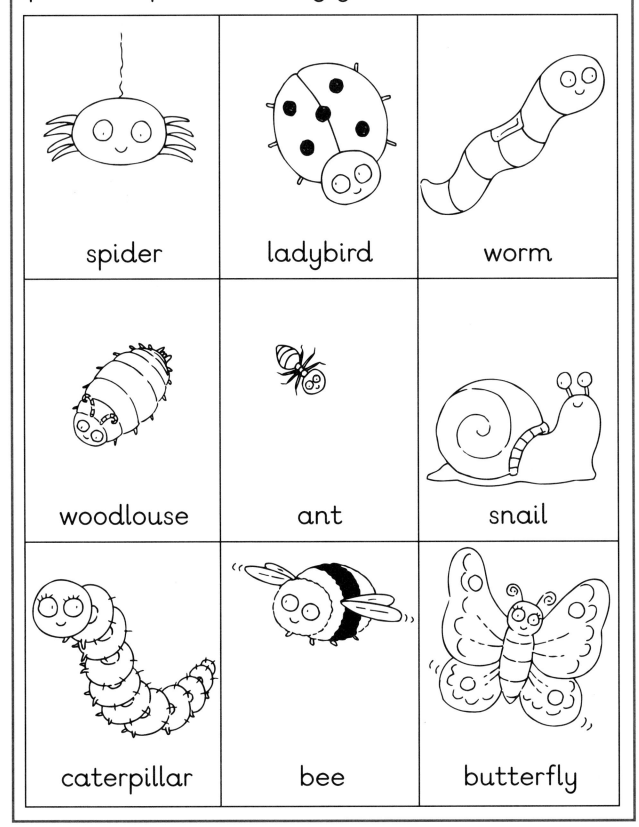

spider	ladybird	worm
woodlouse	ant	snail
caterpillar	bee	butterfly

Two little ladybirds

◆ Write or draw on each ladybird.

Friendly ladybird

Bad-tempered ladybird

Beautiful butterfly

◆ Follow the colour code.

r ➜ red   b ➜ blue   y ➜ yellow   g ➜ green

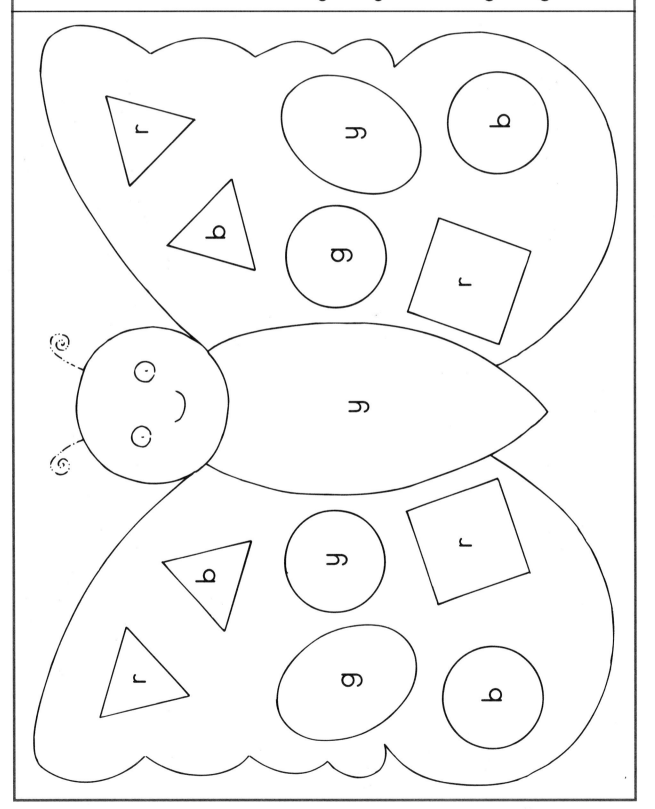

Ugly bug ball

◆ Write your invitation to a friend or toy. Colour in the picture.

To _____

You are invited to an
Ugly Bug Ball

On _____

From _____

Minibeast story book

◆ Choose a minibeast to draw and write about.

I can see you.

A book by

_____

_in_ the grass

_on_ a log

under a leaf

Hungry caterpillars

◆ Colour in and cut out the caterpillars.

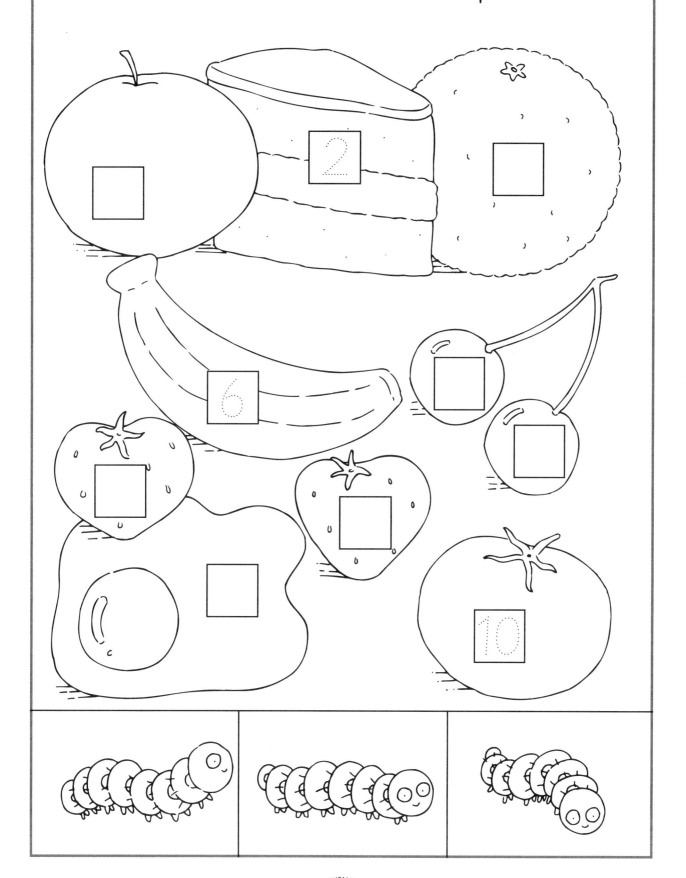

How many spots?

◆ Count the spots and write the answers in the boxes. Use the number line to help you.

| 1 | 2 | 3 | 4 | 5 | 6 | 7 | 8 | 9 | 10 |

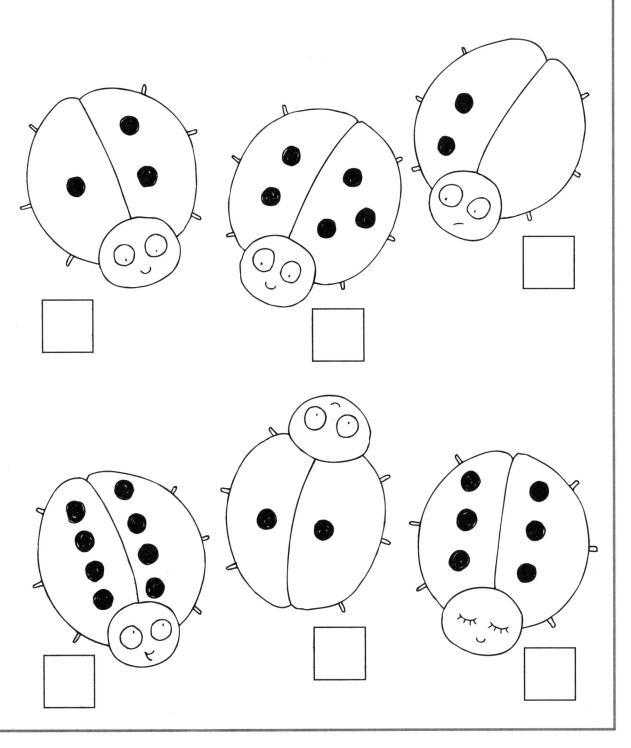

Worms!

◆ Draw each worm a partner who is the same length.

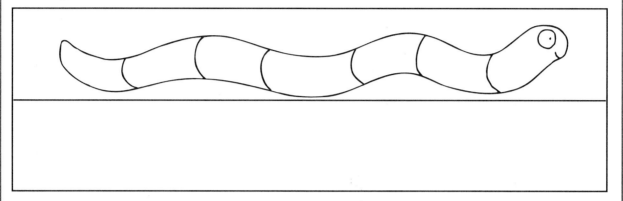

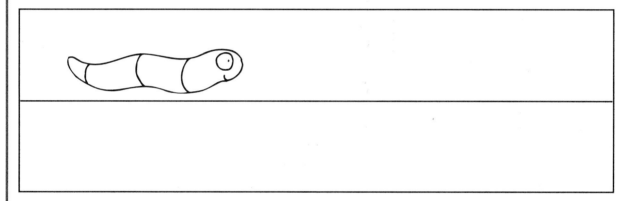

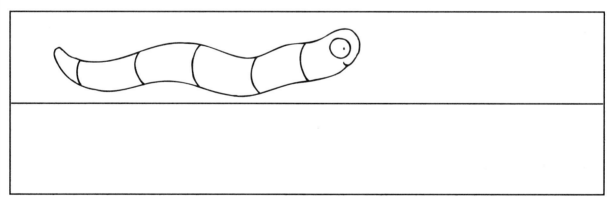

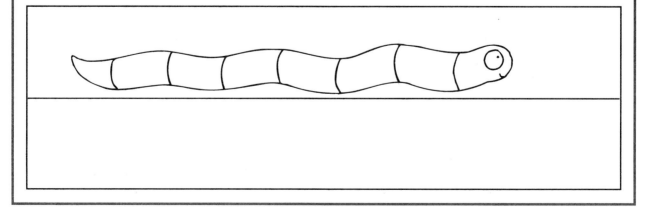

Minibeast hunt

◆ Make these pages into a book.

I am _____

I saw _____

It looked like this

It was _____

I saw it here

Honey-bee puppet

◆ Colour in and cut out the honey-bee. Tape on wings and legs. Hang your puppet up.

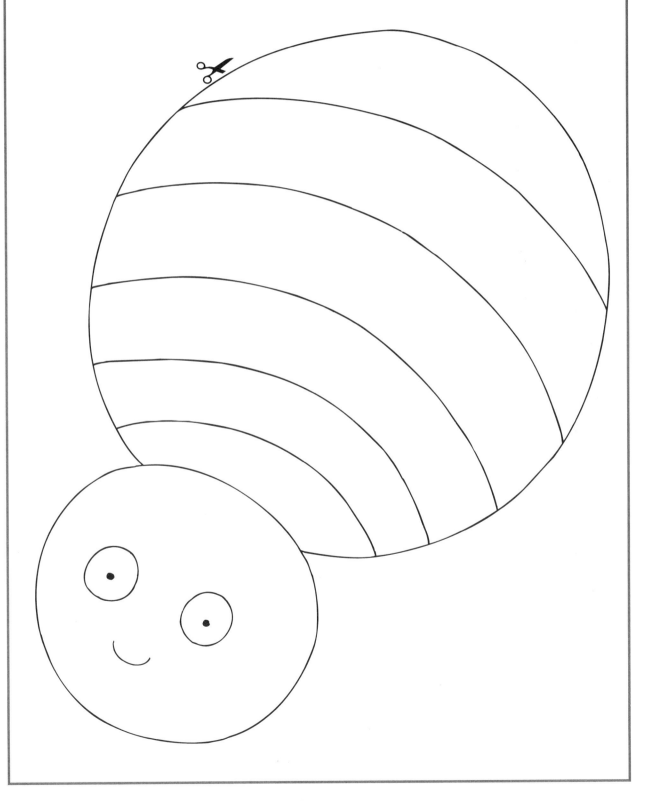

Imaginary minibeast

◆ Decorate and cut out the mask. Tape it onto a headband.

Jazzy caterpillar

◆ Use different coloured pencils to follow the dotted lines. Cut out your caterpillar.

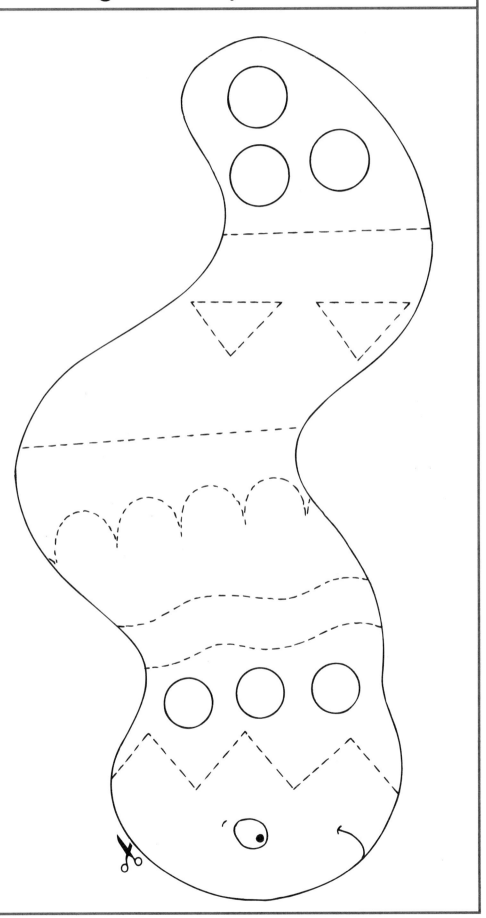

Hiding in the hedgerow

◆ Colour in the picture. Cut out a small photograph of yourself to hide in the picture.

Cut out this leaf
to make a flap
to hide behind.

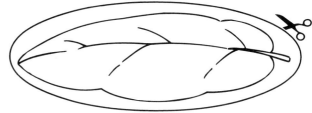

Honeycomb collage

◆ Fill each shape with a different pattern or colour.

Snails

◆ Use a pencil to follow the dotted lines on the snails. Decorate the snails.

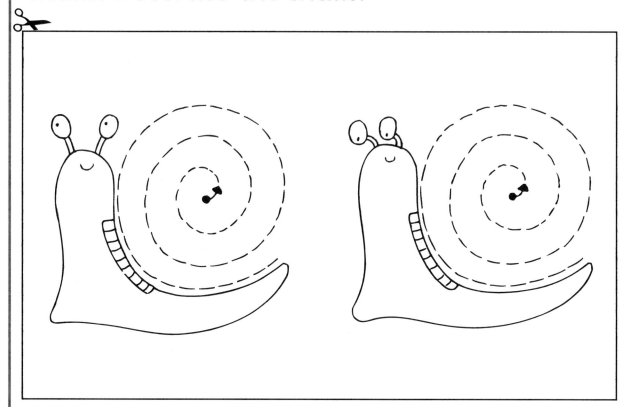

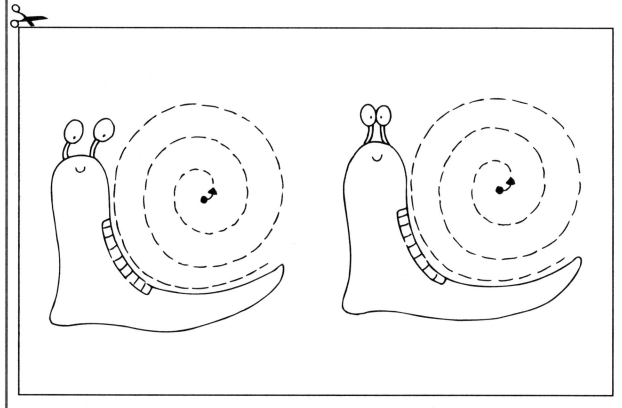

MATERIALS

PAGE 82
TEXTURE GAME

Learning objective
To be sensitive to the challenges faced by people who are unable to see.
(Personal, Social and Emotional Development)
Group size
Small groups to make the games; individuals or pairs to play the game.

Provide each child with a copy of the photocopiable sheet, some glue and a selection of material scraps which fit the descriptions on the sheet – smooth, rough, fluffy and bumpy.

Help the children to stick a small sample of each material in the appropriate box on their sheet and to collect a matching sample of each material to put into an envelope.

How to play: Invite the children to position their texture sheet in front of them and to close their eyes while you hand them one material sample from their envelope. Ask them to use their sense of touch to match the sample to their sheet. Repeat with the other samples. As this is a game of 'self-challenge' there is no need for a winner.

PAGE 83
DRESSING UP

Learning objective
To form good relationships with peers and to work together harmoniously.
(Personal, Social and Emotional Development)
Group size
Pairs of children.

Copy the photocopiable sheet to A4 or A3 and give one sheet to each child. Provide a range of material swatches. Encourage the children to ask their partner to choose their favourite fabrics and colours from the selection provided. Invite each child to dress the person on their sheet in the fabrics and colours chosen by their partner.

Help younger children to cut the fabric to size. Encourage older children to think about their partner's favourite styles such as long or short skirt, shorts or trousers, wide sleeves or narrow sleeves and so on.

PAGE 84
THE WOOLLY SHEEP

Copy the photocopiable sheet and give one to each child. Provide PVA glue (washable), scissors and a selection of coloured wool. Invite the children to give their sheep a colourful woolly coat by cutting and sticking the wool onto the outline of the sheep.

Display several sheep pictures together and encourage the children to describe the colours and the similarities and differences between each picture. Alternatively, encourage the children to play a listening game by taking turns to describe one of the sheep for their peers to identify.

Learning objective
To develop descriptive language.
(Language and Literacy)
Group size
Small groups.

PAGE 85
PATCHWORK QUILT

Give each child a copy of the photocopiable sheet, and six squares of sticky paper or fabric (approximately 15cm by 15cm). Provide glue and a dice to share.

How to play: The first player throws the dice. If, say, 3 is thrown, then that player should cover space number 3 on their quilt using one of their squares of paper or fabric. If space number 3 is already covered, they miss a turn. The dice is then passed to the next player.

The winner is the first player to cover all six spaces on their quilt.

Learning objective
To identify and match numbers 1 to 6.
(Mathematics)
Group size
A game for two players.

PAGE 86
REPEATED PATTERNS

Learning objective
To talk about, recognize and recreate simple patterns to complete a sequence. (Mathematics)
Group size
Small groups.

Give each child a copy of the photocopiable sheet. Talk about the patterns on each strip of wallpaper. Ask the children to finish the patterns by following the sequence. Help younger children by pointing to the shapes, one at a time, as they copy the sequence.

Invite older children to make up their own repeated patterns on strips of paper, to use as wallpaper in 'rooms' made from cardboard boxes.

PAGE 87
MADE FROM WOOD

Learning objective
To gain an awareness of some of the features of objects they observe. (Knowledge and Understanding of the World)
Group size
Small groups.

Provide each child with a copy of the photocopiable sheet and a variety of items made from wood such as different types of paper, lolly sticks, headless matchsticks, old pencils and small building bricks. Invite the children to tape a selection of objects onto their sheet. Use the activity to inspire an interest in how trees are turned into so many different things. Use books and pictures to help explain the process in simple terms.

Challenge older children by including items not made from wood for them to sort out.

PAGE 88
HATS!

Learning objective
To explore and identify the properties of different materials. (Knowledge and Understanding of the World)
Group size
Small groups.

Provide each child with a copy of the photocopiable sheet, scissors, PVA glue (washable) and a selection of contrasting fabrics, such as fine cotton and felt or fur fabric.

Help the children to identify which fabrics would be most suitable for hot days and cold days. Invite them to cut out and glue two hat shapes on their sheet; one for the hot picture and one for the cold picture. Older children could also identify waterproof fabrics to create a rainy day picture.

PAGE 89
NATURAL MATERIALS

Learning objectives
To use a variety of tools and techniques to make a pressed-flower card; to adapt and evaluate their work as necessary. (Knowledge and Understanding of the World)
Group size
Small groups.

Demonstrate how to press flowers and leaves using a flower press or by placing them between two sheets of sugar paper and weighing them down with a heavy object. When the flowers and leaves are pressed, give each child a copy of the photocopiable sheet and invite them to arrange them inside the oval. Let them move the pieces around until they are happy with their design, then glue them down. Laminate the finished pictures. Help the children to write the name of the person that they are sending their card to, and their own name at the bottom. Encourage older children to write a message on the back.

PAGE 90
MATERIAL HUNT

Learning objective
To investigate objects in their everyday environment. (Knowledge and Understanding of the World)
Group size
Individuals or small groups.

Provide each child with a copy of the photocopiable sheet and ensure that all six items are visible within the room. Invite the children to place their sheet onto a clipboard and to carry it around as they 'hunt' for the six items. Explain that they should tick the appropriate box as they 'find' each item.

Turn the activity into a game for older children by giving them a time limit to complete the sheet.

PAGE 91
FLOATING AND SINKING

Learning objective
To ask questions about why things happen. (Knowledge and Understanding of the World)
Group size
Small groups.

Prepare for the activity by finding two familiar objects which float and two which sink. Provide the children with a water tray, aprons and the four objects. Challenge them to find out which objects float and which sink. Encourage them to ask questions as they investigate the objects. To follow up the activity, give each child a copy of the photocopiable sheet and ask them to record their results by drawing the four objects in the correct columns.

PAGE 92
JEWELS ON THE CROWN

arning
jectives
• use
magination in
t and design
• make a
ecorated
own; to wear
eir crowns to
spire mime or
ama.
hysical
evelopment)
roup size
nall groups.

Provide each child with a copy of the photocopiable sheet, strong glue and a range of shiny and decorative materials such as buttons, beads, glitter, shiny paper, gold and silver pens or crayons, sequins, shiny fabric, ribbon and braid. Invite the children to cut out their crown shape and decorate it with the materials. Make a headband for each child using a strip of card and help them to attach their crown to the band.

Invite the children to wear their crowns while re-enacting rhymes such as, 'The Queen of Hearts', 'Sing a Song of Sixpence' and 'Old King Cole', or during imaginative role-play.

PAGE 93
DECORATING

arning
bjective
• use
anipulative
ills to print a
esign, cut
bric to size
nd arrange
ctures
urposefully.
hysical
evelopment)
roup size
dividuals or
nall groups.

Provide each child with a copy of the photocopiable sheet (enlarged if possible) and a range of printing materials.

Invite the children to 'decorate' the room on the sheet using their own choice of patterns and colours.

When dry, encourage the children to cut and stick small pieces of fabric at the window and on the floor to represent curtains and carpet. Provide magazines or catalogues containing furniture pictures and invite the children to cut out items of furniture to arrange in their room.

PAGE 95
SPECIAL GIFT-WRAPPING

Provide each child with a copy of the photocopiable sheet (enlarged if possible). Talk about the gift that teddy is holding, and ask the children who they think it might be for. How could it be wrapped to make it look special?

Provide a wide range of decorative materials such as ribbons, small bows and samples of wrapping paper, and invite the children to use them to decorate the parcel.

Encourage the children to write their name on the label to say who the imaginary gift is from.

**Learning
objective**
To use
decorative
materials to
inspire creative
imagination.
(Creative
Development)
Group size
Individuals or
small groups.

PAGE 94
SHINY ROBOT

arning
bjective
• use a range
materials to
eate a 2-D
bot picture.
reative
evelopment)
roup size
dividuals or
nall groups.

Provide each child with a copy of the photocopiable sheet (enlarged if possible) and a range of shiny paper and coloured foil, such as tin foil and sweet wrappings.

Encourage the children to use their imaginations to create a shiny robot on their sheet. When complete, position several robots in a line along a display board, and add a number label to each robot to create an unusual number line. Alternatively, secure the robots back to back and hang in the light to create eye-catching mobiles.

PAGE 96
BUILD A LIGHTHOUSE

Read the story *The Lighthouse Keeper's Lunch* by Ronda and David Armitage (Hippo). From a selection of junk materials, encourage the children to choose their own materials to build a model of the lighthouse. Invite them to paint their model in their own choice of colours.

When complete, provide each child with a copy of the photocopiable sheet, and ask them to draw a picture of their model lighthouse. Invite them to colour their picture using colours to match their model.

**Learning
objective**
To select
appropriate
materials to
construct a
simple model.
(Creative
Development)
Group size
Small groups.

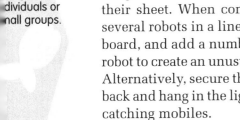

Texture game

◆ Choose five materials to stick in each box.

smooth	rough
fluffy	bumpy

Dressing up

◆ Cut up some material and glue it onto the person to dress them.

The woolly sheep

◆ Give the sheep a colourful, woolly coat.

My woolly sheep, by _____

Patchwork quilt

◆ Throw a dice and cover the squares.

Repeated patterns

♦ Finish the patterns on the wallpaper.

Made from wood

◆ Fill the tree with things made from wood.

Things made from wood.
By:

_____

Hats!

◆ Use different materials to make two hats.

A hot day

A cold day

Natural materials

◆ Glue some leaves or flowers in the oval.

To_____

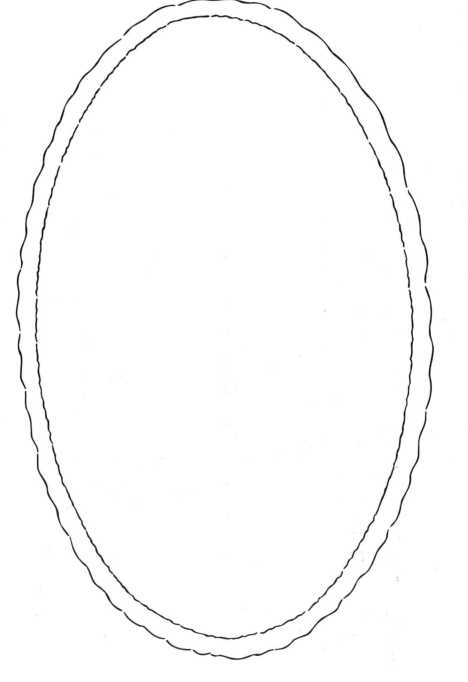

From_____

Material hunt

◆ Look around you. Tick the boxes when you find each item.

wool ☐

plastic ☐

glass ☐

paper ☐

wood ☐

fabric ☐

Floating and sinking

◆ Draw two things which float and two things which sink.

Floats	Sinks

Jewels on the crown

◆ Decorate and cut out the crown. Make a headband and glue your crown onto it.

Decorating

◆ Use printing materials to decorate this room. Add fabric curtains and carpet.

Shiny robot

◆ Use tin foil or shiny paper to decorate the robot.

Special gift-wrapping

◆ Decorate the parcel and write your name on the label.

From
_____

Build a lighthouse

◆ Draw a picture of your model lighthouse.
Colour it in.

Name: _____